CH0066207£

Francis Frith's
Padstow

BRIAN PEARCE is Research and Information Officer for Exmoor National Park Authority and spends much time researching facts and figures about that area and the West Country as a whole. In addition, he is a freelance writer, photographer, lecturer and guide. He has written a variety of books on West Country themes, including the Minehead book in this series, and has contributed many walks and town trails in Cornwall to national publications. He has spent much time exploring the coast of north Cornwall and has an intimate knowledge of Padstow.

Photographic Memories

Francis Frith's
Padstow

Brian Pearce

First published in the United Kingdom in 2002 by
Frith Book Company Ltd

Paperback Edition 2002
ISBN 1-85937-641-x

Text and Design copyright © Frith Book Company Ltd
Photographs copyright © The Francis Frith Collection

The Frith photographs and the Frith logo are reproduced under licence from
Heritage Photographic Resources Ltd, the owners of the Frith archive and trademarks

All rights reserved. No photograph in this publication may be sold to a third party other than in
the original form of this publication, or framed for sale to a third party.
No parts of this publication may be reproduced, stored in a retrieval system, or
transmitted, in any form, or by any means, electronic, mechanical, photocopying, recording or
otherwise, without the prior permission of the publishers and copyright holder.

British Library Cataloguing in Publication Data

Francis Frith's Padstow
Brian Pearce

Frith Book Company Ltd
Frith's Barn, Teffont,
Salisbury, Wiltshire SP3 5QP
Tel: +44 (0) 1722 716 376
Email: info@francisfrith.co.uk
www.francisfrith.co.uk

Printed and bound in Great Britain

Front Cover: Padstow, The Harbour 1901 47714

AS WITH ANY HISTORICAL DATABASE THE FRITH ARCHIVE IS CONSTANTLY BEING CORRECTED AND IMPROVED
AND THE PUBLISHERS WOULD WELCOME INFORMATION ON OMISSIONS OR INACCURACIES

Contents

Francis Frith: *Victorian Pioneer*

FRANCIS FRITH, Victorian founder of the world-famous photographic archive, was a complex and multi-talented man. A devout Quaker and a highly successful Victorian businessman, he was both philosophic by nature and pioneering in outlook.

By 1855 Francis Frith had already established a wholesale grocery business in Liverpool, and sold it for the astonishing sum of £200,000, which is the equivalent today of over £15,000,000. Now a multi-millionaire, he was able to indulge his passion for travel. As a child he had pored over travel books written by early explorers, and his fancy and imagination had been stirred by family holidays to the sublime mountain regions of Wales and Scotland. 'What a land of spirit-stirring and enriching scenes and places!' he had written. He was to return to these scenes of grandeur in later years to 'recapture the thousands of vivid and tender memories', but with a different purpose. Now in his thirties, and captivated by the new science of photography, Frith set out on a series of pioneering journeys to the Nile regions that occupied him from 1856 until 1860.

Intrigue and Adventure

He took with him on his travels a specially-designed wicker carriage that acted as both dark-room and sleeping chamber. These far-flung journeys were packed with intrigue and adventure. In his life story, written when he was sixty-three, Frith tells of being held captive by bandits, and of fighting 'an awful midnight battle to the very point of surrender with a deadly pack of hungry, wild dogs'. Sporting flowing Arab costume, Frith arrived at Akaba by camel seventy years before Lawrence, where he encountered 'desert princes and rival sheikhs, blazing with jewel-hilted swords'.

During these extraordinary adventures he was assiduously exploring the desert regions bordering the Nile and patiently recording the antiquities and peoples with his camera. He was the first photographer to venture beyond the sixth cataract. Africa was still the mysterious 'Dark Continent', and Stanley and Livingstone's historic meeting was a decade into the future. The conditions for picture taking confound belief. He laboured for hours in his wicker dark-room in the sweltering heat of the desert, while the volatile chemicals fizzed dangerously in their trays. Often he was forced to work in remote tombs and caves where conditions were cooler. Back in London he exhibited his photographs and was 'rapturously cheered' by members of the Royal Society. His reputation as a photographer was made overnight. An eminent modern historian has likened their impact on the population of the time to that on our own generation of the first photographs taken on the surface of the moon.

Venture of a Life-Time

Characteristically, Frith quickly spotted the opportunity to create a new business as a specialist publisher of photographs. He lived in an era of immense and sometimes violent change. For the poor in the early part of Victoria's reign work was a drudge and the hours long, and people had precious little free time to enjoy themselves. Most had no transport other than a cart or gig at their disposal, and had not travelled far beyond the boundaries of their own town or village. However, by the

1870s, the railways had threaded their way across the country, and Bank Holidays and half-day Saturdays had been made obligatory by Act of Parliament. All of a sudden the ordinary working man and his family were able to enjoy days out and see a little more of the world.

With characteristic business acumen, Francis Frith foresaw that these new tourists would enjoy having souvenirs to commemorate their days out. In 1860 he married Mary Ann Rosling and set out with the intention of photographing every city, town and village in Britain. For the next thirty years he travelled the country by train and by pony and trap, producing fine photographs of seaside resorts and beauty spots that were keenly bought by millions of Victorians. These prints were painstakingly pasted into family albums and pored over during the dark nights of winter, rekindling precious memories of summer excursions.

The Rise of Frith & Co

Frith's studio was soon supplying retail shops all over the country. To meet the demand he gathered about him a small team of photographers, and published the work of independent artist-photographers of the calibre of Roger Fenton and Francis Bedford. In order to gain some understanding of the scale of Frith's business one only has to look at the catalogue issued by Frith & Co in 1886: it runs to some 670 pages, listing not only many thousands of views of the British Isles but also many photographs of most European countries, and China, Japan, the USA and Canada – note the sample page shown above from the hand-written *Frith & Co* ledgers detailing pictures taken. By 1890 Frith had created the greatest specialist photographic publishing company in the world, with over 2,000

became the standard format, but it was not until 1902 that the divided back came into being, with address and message on one face and a full-size illustration on the other. *Frith & Co* were in the vanguard of postcard development, and Frith's sons Eustace and Cyril continued their father's monumental task, expanding the number of views offered to the public and recording more and more places in Britain, as the coasts and countryside were opened up to mass travel.

Francis Frith died in 1898 at his villa in Cannes, his great project still growing. The archive he created continued in business for another seventy years. By 1970 it contained over a third of a million pictures of 7,000 cities, towns and villages. The massive photographic record Frith has left to us stands as a living monument to a special and very remarkable man.

outlets – more than the combined number that Boots and WH Smith have today! The picture on the right shows the *Frith & Co* display board at Ingleton in the Yorkshire Dales. Beautifully constructed with mahogany frame and gilt inserts, it could display up to a dozen local scenes.

Postcard Bonanza

The ever-popular holiday postcard we know today took many years to develop. In 1870 the Post Office issued the first plain cards, with a pre-printed stamp on one face. In 1894 they allowed other publishers' cards to be sent through the mail with an attached adhesive halfpenny stamp. Demand grew rapidly, and in 1895 a new size of postcard was permitted called the court card, but there was little room for illustration. In 1899, a year after Frith's death, a new card measuring 5.5 x 3.5 inches

Frith's Archive: *A Unique Legacy*

FRANCIS FRITH'S legacy to us today is of immense significance and value, for the magnificent archive of evocative photographs he created provides a unique record of change in 7,000 cities, towns and villages throughout Britain over a century and more. Frith and his fellow studio photographers revisited locations many times down the years to update their views, compiling for us an enthralling and colourful pageant of British life and character.

We tend to think of Frith's sepia views of Britain as nostalgic, for most of us use them to conjure up memories of places in our own lives with which we have family associations. It often makes us forget that to Francis Frith they were records of daily life as it was actually being lived in the cities, towns and villages of his day. The Victorian age was one of great and often bewildering change for ordinary people, and though the pictures evoke an impres-

sion of slower times, life was as busy and hectic as it is today.

We are fortunate that Frith was a photographer of the people, dedicated to recording the minutiae of everyday life. For it is this sheer wealth of visual data, the painstaking chronicle of changes in dress, transport, street layouts, buildings, housing, engineering and landscape that captivates us so much today. His remarkable images offer us a powerful link with the past and with the lives of our ancestors.

Today's Technology

Computers have now made it possible for Frith's many thousands of images to be accessed almost instantly. In the Frith archive today, each photograph is carefully 'digitised' then stored on a CD Rom. Frith archivists can locate a single photograph amongst thousands within seconds. Views can be catalogued and sorted under a variety of categories of place and content to the immediate benefit of researchers.

Inexpensive reference prints can be created for them at the touch of a mouse button, and a wide range of books and other printed materials assembled and published for a wider, more general readership - in the next twelve months over a hundred Frith local history titles will be published! The day-to-day workings of the archive are very different from how they were in Francis Frith's time: imagine the herculean task of sorting through eleven tons of glass negatives as Frith had to do to locate a particular sequence of pictures! Yet the archive still

THE FRANCIS FRITH COLLECTION
Photographic publishers since 1860

HOME | PHOTO SEARCH | BOOKS | PORTFOLIO | GALLERY | MY CART
Products | History | Other Collections | Contact us | Help?

your town,
your village

365,000 photographs of 7,000 towns and villages, taken between 1860 & 1970.

The Frith Archive
The Frith Archive is the remarkable legacy of its energetic and visionary founder. Today, the Frith archive is the only nationally important archive of its kind still in private ownership.

The Collection is world-renowned for the extraordinary quality of its images.

The Gallery
This month The Frith Gallery features images from "Frith's Egypt".

News...
Image update complete. An additional 5,000 images have been added and the quality of all images has now been improved.

Sample Chapters available. The first selection of sample chapters from the Frith Book Co.'s extensive range is now available. All are offered in Pdf format for easy downloading and viewing.

explore FRITH
Search thousands of photographs from one of the worlds' great archives.

Town search
[   ] GO

County search
[Select a county ▾] GO

the FRITHgallery

See Frith at www.francisfrith.co.uk

prides itself on maintaining the same high standards of excellence laid down by Francis Frith, including the painstaking cataloguing and indexing of every view.

It is curious to reflect on how the internet now allows researchers in America and elsewhere greater instant access to the archive than Frith himself ever enjoyed. Many thousands of individual views can be called up on screen within seconds on one of the Frith internet sites, enabling people living continents away to revisit the streets of their ancestral home town, or view places in Britain where they have enjoyed holidays. Many overseas researchers welcome the chance to view special theme selections, such as transport, sports, costume and ancient monuments.

We are certain that Francis Frith would have heartily approved of these modern developments in imaging techniques, for he himself was always working at the very limits of Victorian photographic technology.

The Value of the Archive Today

Because of the benefits brought by the computer, Frith's images are increasingly studied by social historians, by researchers into genealogy and ancestory, by architects, town planners, and by teachers and schoolchildren involved in local history projects.

In addition, the archive offers every one of us an opportunity to examine the places where we and our families have lived and worked down the years. Highly successful in Frith's own era, the archive is now, a century and more on, entering a new phase of popularity.

The Past in Tune with the Future

Historians consider the Francis Frith Collection to be of prime national importance. It is the only archive of its kind remaining in private ownership and has been valued at a million pounds. However, this figure is now rapidly increasing as digital technology enables more and more people around the world to enjoy its benefits.

Francis Frith's archive is now housed in an historic timber barn in the beautiful village of Teffont in Wiltshire. Its founder would not recognize the archive office as it is today. In place of the many thousands of dusty boxes containing glass plate negatives and an all-pervading odour of photographic chemicals, there are now ranks of computer screens. He would be amazed to watch his images travelling round the world at unimaginable speeds through network and internet lines.

The archive's future is both bright and exciting. Francis Frith, with his unshakeable belief in making photographs available to the greatest number of people, would undoubtedly approve of what is being done today with his lifetime's work. His photographs, depicting our shared past, are now bringing pleasure and enlightenment to millions around the world a century and more after his death.

The Quay 1910
69710

The Cornish called Padstow Lodenek, but the Saxons renamed it Petrockstowe after St Petroc. He is reputed to have been a Welsh prince who shunned his inheritance to learn Christianity in Ireland. Determined to preach the Gospel, he crossed to Padstow in 518, where Bishop Wethinoc was already converting the locals to Christianity, and founded a monastery there. From his base at Bodmin he and his monks travelled widely both in the West Country and abroad. He is said to have died at Treroval near Padstow, where he was buried. Following Viking coastal raids in 981, his bones and the Padstow monastery were moved to Bodmin.

Petrockstowe became 'Attest' in English, possibly after King Athelstan, who gave it privileges; or perhaps the name was a corruption of Adelstowe, after a local bishop. It certainly had the privilege of sanctuary until the Middle Ages, which meant that law-breakers could escape punishment by staying within the Liberty of St Petroc, which included most of the town. This gave the place a bad reputation.

The Domesday Book records that all of Attest belonged to the church. Medieval Attest belonged to Bodmin Priory. The Abbot collected tithes from the harbour, which was en route for pilgrims travelling from Ireland and Wales to Rome. They would travel overland to

The View from the Sands 1888 21200

This view is unusual in that it was taken from the sands which are uncovered at low tide in the middle of the estuary. It is an early photograph, showing how the settlement was largely confined to the valley, which was a former creek of the estuary. To the left of the settlement are shipyards which were gone when the railway arrived ten years later.

The Abbey House 1906 56269

The Abbey House stands on the North Quay. It has carved stonework which may have come from a religious building, and it is said to have been a monastery, a nunnery or a priest's house. Others say it was the port Toll House or Custom House for Bodmin Priory. It is more likely that it was once the Guild House of medieval merchants. The Guild of St Petroc was formed by local traders to finance fishing ventures. The large round objects behind the railings are said to have been 'cloam' (clay) ovens, which were built into the backs of fireplaces and fired by wood.

St Michael's Mount or Fowey for boats to the continent. The Saints Way footpath now commemorates their route. It was also a pack horse and trading route, which was possibly established before 2000BC as part of a route from France to Fowey, Padstow and Ireland for carrying precious metals. The Romans are thought to have used Padstow as a centre for trading minerals throughout their empire.

There is a legend that the Abbey House (56269, page 15) was linked with the monastery by a tunnel. After Prideaux Place occupied the site of the monastery, the tunnel was said to have been used by the future Charles II during the Civil War to escape from the Place to the harbour and thence to France. The town supported Parliament, and Edmund Prideaux was Secretary General to Oliver Cromwell. However, he carefully avoided signing the death warrant of Charles I and maintained friendships with Royalists. The family was given a royal pardon after the Restoration, but this was probably due to the influence of the then Secretary of State, Sir William Morice, who had married a Prideaux.

The port sent two ships to the siege of Calais in 1344, and more to fight the Armada in 1588, by which time it was known as Padstow. Tin, hides, herrings and pilchards were exported, and woollens, salt and canvas were imported. Padstow declined in importance in the time of Henry VIII through the partial silting up of the harbour and continual piracy. Elizabeth I granted the town borough status for its endeavours in the defence of the realm, but the Prideaux family, fearing a reduction in their status as Lords of the Manor, managed to have this honour removed. Trade revived in the mid 18th century with the export of copper, but this was soon taken over by St Ives. Leland said that

Padstow was 'a good quick fisher town but uncleanly kept'. He said that in early days small boats came from Brittany, landing at high tide to buy fish and exchange goods. He also said that the town was full of Irish men, and Carew, in his Survey of Cornwall, said that its greatest trade was with Ireland.

Defoe, writing in 1724, also mentioned the Irish trade. He noted that it was the nearest safe

From the Deer Park 1894
33575

The picture was probably taken from Stile Field, next to the Deer Park. The latter belongs to Prideaux Place, and is connected to it by an arch over the road, in front of the house. It is said to be the oldest deer park in Britain - there is evidence to date it back to the last days of Roman Britain in 435AD. The present park dates from the landscaping of 1750, although fallow deer were mentioned here as early as 1170. The park still contains fallow deer; it is said that if the deer ever leave the Place, the Prideaux family will also leave.

haven before Ireland, and that in good conditions the journey took only twenty-four hours. Pococke, writing in 1750, said that the Irish trade was for corn, while the imports from Ireland were glass, linen, salted pork and tallow. Linen also came from Brittany, along with salt, wine and vinegar. There was also trade with Bristol for many goods, including cured fish, and with Wales for coal and with the export of slate. The expansion of mining meant that ores of copper, lead and antimony were exported, as well as tin. Maton, writing in 1794-96, said that the harbour was so much obstructed by sand that navigation was difficult, although large ships could sail up the main channel of the Camel. Wadebridge was still a substantial port. According to legend, the harbour was cursed by a mermaid who was

View over the Harbour 1894 33573

On top of the hill to the right stands Dennis Farm, which later became an hotel; it is now a residential home for the elderly. To its left is Dennis Hill, the name of which probably comes from the Cornish 'dinas', meaning a fort, suggesting that a hill fort may have stood there before the erection of the Jubilee Obelisk, three years after the picture was taken.

shot with a longbow by a greedy Padstow man. She cast some sand into the sea, and foretold that it would block the harbour.

Until the late 19th century, most transport was by sea, for Cornwall was isolated in terms of inland communications. The main route outwards roughly parallelled the present A39, but it ran through Padstow. This explains the presence of the old London Inn, where horses were available for the journey. The first turnpike road - from Wadebridge - came in 1760. The Napoleonic Wars meant reduced trade with the continent, resulting in poverty in Padstow and food riots in 1810. A workhouse for the poor was operated between 1768 and 1842. About 5% of the population died of cholera in 1850, and cholera and typhus struck again later in the century. Main drains were installed in 1867 by Charles Prideaux-Brune, who was moved by the deaths of so many children.

Despite the poverty, it was the 19th century which saw the harbour's busiest times. Timber was brought in from Scandinavia and Canada, and emigrants to the New World returned on the same ships. The larger ships moored in the Pool, a deep water anchorage beyond the harbour. There were smacks, schooners, brigs, brigantines, barquentines and square riggers. The town had five shipyards in the mid 19th century, building mostly topsail schooners, but they did not survive long after iron and steam ships became fashionable. The last wooden schooner was launched in 1887. Three remaining yards made small fishing boats. There is a new boat yard by the old railway yard.

The coming of the railway contributed to the decline of the coastal shipping trade, although it helped with the fishing industry in getting fresh fish to Billingsgate. A railway came to Wadebridge from Bodmin in 1834, passing into

the hands of the London and South Western Railway in 1847; several branch lines were added to that railway's network before Padstow was eventually connected to Wadebridge in 1899. By that time, Padstow had become run down, and tourism took a while to develop. In a guide book of the period, C S Ward stated: 'We imagine few deliberately visit Padstow for its own sake'. Murray's Guide described it as 'one of those antiquated unsavoury fishing towns best viewed from a distance'.

The line became part of the Southern Railway in 1923, and then British Railways upon nationalisation in 1948. The Atlantic Coast Express brought holidaymakers from Waterloo to Padstow from 1926 until 1964 - the journey took 6 hours 21 minutes. During the Depression, the resort attracted the affluent of London's south-western suburbs; the London newspapers went ahead of them by freight train, and buses would meet the trains at the station. E P Leigh-Bennett wrote about resorts served by the express. Arriving at Padstow in the 1930s, he wrote: 'The train wriggled round a bend and its engine shrieked joyfully, as well it might, for the evening sun was kissing the grey roof tops of Padstow which sits deep set in a corner of the hills ahead, and the sight of it was very lovely'. Another writer who used the train was S P B Mais, who found Padstow 'an ancient place of narrow, crooked alleys and palm trees and fuchsias growing in every garden'. After the Second World War less affluent visitors were able to come, attracted by caravan sites and chalets.

Padstow's population grew from 1,546 in 1901 to about 2,500 when the railway closed in 1967, and then hardly grew at all. Diesel units were introduced on the line in 1965, a year before the Beeching axe which closed many branch lines.

View over the Town and the Harbour 1894 33574

This picture and 33547a (page 22) form a panoramic view over the town and harbour. They show the number of private gardens in the town in the late 19th century. In the foreground are the walled gardens of St Petroc's House, which dates from 1710. In the early 19th century it was owned by the Rawlings family, local bankers, who ran into financial difficulties. It later became an hotel, now in the ownership of Rick Stein. Across the valley, below St Saviour's Lane, are other walled gardens belonging to wealthy families It seems that as one became more important one moved physically higher up in the town, with the Prideaux family at the top.

Wadebridge continued to receive freight traffic from Bodmin until 1978. The Camel Trail footpath and cycleway now follows the line. The closing of the railway nearly finished off the fishing industry, which began to decline after the Second World War. However, the catching of shellfish, particularly crabs and lobsters, grew in importance in the 1980s. Television chef Rick Stein has boosted the popularity of seafish, and he has put Padstow on the map. His commercial outlets have multiplied to the point where some are calling the town 'Padstein'. Let us hope that this interest in seafish will not be a short lived fashion.

Houses were built for the armed forces during the Second World War, and council estates were built afterwards. Many who came on holiday here in their childhood returned to live here in their retirement, and there has been much building at Port Arthur, Dennis Lane, Dennis

Cove, Sarah's View, Rainy Field and Chaddlewood. However, there are still many old local families in the area.

The town now has many tourist shops, flats and art galleries. It is still best known for its ancient May Day hobby horse celebrations. The 'Oss is a man dressed in a heavy costume with snapping jaws, plumed cap and hooped skirt. He is accompanied by a Teaser, singers, dancers and musicians who revive him at intervals. The 'Oss is thought to be a fertility symbol and a woman 'caught' under its skirts is supposed to become lucky or pregnant. The ancient custom starts at midnight on 30 April and continues until 2 May.

Since the First World War there have been two horses. They emerge from their 'stables' on May Day morning, and are supported by locals wearing white, a buttonhole of spring flowers and a red or blue ribbon according to the 'Oss. Traditional songs are sung until the evening, and maypole dancing follows the day after. The ceremony contributes to the general liveliness of Padstow today.

Cornwall is one of the most deprived parts of the country. Tourism brings employment, but wages are low, and many jobs are part time or seasonal. Despite this, the town does not feel depressed, and seems to be undergoing a revival. Long may it last.

View over the Town 1894 33574a

St Petroc's Church, the Interior 1888 21209

This picture shows the nave and chancel. In the foreground is a 14th-century font decorated with figures of the twelve apostles. It is made of slatey catacleuse stone from Trevose Head. John Betjeman described the stone as 'the only slate which can be deeply carved, it is of blue-grey colour and has a look of cast iron'. There was a superstition that nobody baptised in the font would be hung. This ended when James Elliot was hung for robbing the mail in 1787.

The parish church is dedicated to St Petroc. According to legend, he crossed from Ireland on a cabbage leaf; apparently, some old Irish boats were actually made from strong leaves. Another legend was that he crossed on a stone altar, which was placed in his original church. It would have stood at the end of a small creek, which is now silted up and covered by the old part of the town. This church was destroyed by the Vikings, and a new one was built in the early 12th century. However, this was built of poor stone from the local beach; apart from the base of the tower, it had to be rebuilt. The Early English tower, dating from 1425-1450, is the oldest part of the present church. Better building stone from Caen in Normandy was used, along with local catacleuse stone from Trevose Head. Some building dates from the time of Prior Vivian, the last Prior of Bodmin before the dissolution of the priory in 1538.

The Tudor oak pulpit in the nave (21209, above) is decorated with symbols of the Passion and Crucifixion. Between it and the chancel there is now a rood screen, made in 1900 to replace a long-lost medieval screen. The chancel roof was replaced during the same restoration, and the east window was replaced in 1958. The chancel is thought to cover the original church of St Petroc. In its southern wall, to the right of the altar, there is a canopied rose piscina, on top of which is a figure of a monk, said to be St Petroc. Also to the right of the altar there is now a seat made with bench

St Petroc's Church, from the South 1888 21208

ends taken from medieval pews. One end is carved with a cowled fox preaching to a goose - some say the fox is the Devil in disguise, others that it is a reference to the friars who used to preach there. The seat is now used by visiting clergy. To the left of the altar is a brass dated 1421 to Laurence Merther, the vicar who initiated the rebuilding of the church but did not live to see it.

The churchyard has several entrances, one with a lych gate. Just inside the south-east gate are the remains of a granite Celtic cross, which was found by grave diggers in the 1860s. It is thought to date from the 10th century, when Padstow was the seat of a Cornish bishop. The first such bishop was Adelstan, nominated by Edward the Elder in 905. The bishopric only lasted until 931, when King Athelstan moved it to St Germans. It was later moved to Exeter, and there was no bishropric in Cornwall until its

own cathedral was built at Truro in the 19th century. In the south-west corner of the churchyard is the old town morgue, restored in 1996 and now used as a store.

At the west end of the church, beyond the tower, is a vault for members of the Prideaux family. Over the door is an ancient cross found in the grounds of Prideaux Place. It was placed there in memory of Charles Prideaux-Brune, his wife Frances and daughter Anna, who all died within two years in the 1830s.

Prideaux House (21202, page 28) was built above the church, possibly on the site of the original monastery, or where St Samson lived as a hermit. A religious house was founded thereabouts by St Petroc in 560, and this was burnt by the Vikings in 981. A later monastery was said to have grown around a spring which arose from St Petroc's tomb, and nearby is a lane called Fentonluna, which means a

St Petroc's Church, the Prideaux Monument 1920
69708

There are several monuments to the Prideaux family in the church. The family has lived at Prideaux Place for 14 generations, and 26 generations have lived in the West Country, with links back to William the Conqueror. The picture is of a monument of 1627 to Sir Nicholas Prideaux, builder of Prideaux Place. It depicts Sir Nicholas in armour with his wife and four sons.

springing of water near a church. In the lane is a disused pump and well, inscribed with the name of Prideaux and dated 1592, but it was moved there in the 19th century.

Later it became the site of a grange farm and tithe barn belonging to Bodmin Priory. In anticipation of the dissolution of the monasteries by Henry VIII, two members of a local family, Humphrey and Nicholas Prideaux, advised the Priory to lease their lands and properties to friends at nominal rents. Humphrey Prideaux's son married the Prior's niece, and they were given a 99-year lease on the Manor of Padstow as a wedding present. By a devious route the lease was conveyed to Nicholas Prideaux, successfully avoiding the king's grasp on the property, despite a lawsuit. The Prideauxs took over as Lords of the Manor of Padstow from the Priors of Bodmin, and Prideaux Place became the manor house.

Another Nicholas Prideaux rebuilt the house between 1581 and 1592 in the fashionable E-shape of the age. Daniel Defoe, writing in 1724, said: 'time makes the architect of it look a little out of fashion'. The house underwent considerable alteration in the 18th and 19th centuries, but the front remained largely unaltered. Parts became derelict, and today only 6 of its 46 bedrooms are habitable. Some remain exactly as the American Army left them before D-Day in the Second World War.

In the morning room there are interesting portraits, including several by the 18th-century Cornish artist John Opie. Whilst only a boy, Opie, the son of a carpenter from St Agnes, arrived at the house and proceeded to paint the entire family, including their pets. It is said that he arrived in a plain jacket and left in a fancy coat, lace ruffles and silk stockings, and with 20 guineas in his pocket. He never seemed to look back, and was a successful artist in his day, receiving praise from Sir Joshua Reynolds, alongside whose tomb he now rests in St Paul's.

Church Street 1920 69707

Some of the more important people in the town, such as sea captains and merchants, lived in Church Street.

Above: **St Petroc's Church and Prideaux Place 1888**
21201

Left: **Prideaux Place 1888** 21202

**Prideaux
Place 1903**
49951

In the library is a portrait of Humphrey Prideaux, born at the Place in 1648. As Dean of Norwich he was an academic theologian and author of 'The Connection of the Old and New Testaments'. Although a Church of England clergyman, he received a Gold Medal from the Pope for this work, which is still in the house along with the original manuscript. The family played a major role in Cornish affairs. They added Brune to their name after marriage into that family in 1799. The present owner, Peter Prideaux-Brune, follows a family tradition of becoming lawyers.

The house was built in an elevated position and is surrounded by trees. Trees and parkland are rare in north Cornwall because of the prevailing westerly winds, and the trees here form a shelter belt for the house and gardens. The gardens used to be open to the public only for special events, but in recent years they have been regularly opening in the summer months. Interest has arisen since the Place featured in films and TV series, including 'Twelfth Night' and 'Coming Home'.

The present gardens of Prideaux Place date back to the 1730s, when they were landscaped by Edmund Prideaux. Following a Grand Tour of Europe, he created hedged walks, built a classical temple, grotto and obelisk, and added Roman urns. The grounds already contained

Prideaux Place, the Billiard Room 1888 21205

The billiard room is now a drawing room, renamed the Grenville Room. Originally, the decorations were in the dining room of Sir Richard Grenville at his manor at Stowe in north Cornwall. Stowe was built during the reign of Charles II, but for want of a Grenville heir, it soon fell derelict. Before it was demolished, Edmund Prideaux, who was related to the Grenvilles by marriage, removed the room and its fittings and recreated it at Prideaux Place. The fittings included a mirror with a surround carved by Grinling Gibbons, three paintings by Antonio Verrio and portraits of Charles II, Sir Beville Grenville and John Wilmot, Earl of Rochester.

Prideaux Place, the Hall 1888 21206

The hall is a fine example of Regency Gothic architecture. The staircase is of an earlier period; it came from the Grenville family home of Stowe, and has an intriguing cantilever design, giving it no visible means of support. It runs up to bedrooms and the gallery, with its wonderful Tudor ceiling plastered with biblical themes. To the left of the photograph, steps also run up to the library, which is in a similar Gothic style and with a large collection of rare leather-bound books. Today there are no rugs on the floor, which was painted with a tile design for the filming of 'Twelfth Night'. Against the wall on the right there is now a sea chest inlaid with silver and mother of pearl which came from an Armada ship wrecked off Padstow.

Prideaux Place, the Oak Room 1888 21204

In the Elizabethan house this was the Great Hall, separated from the entrance passage by a carved oak screen which still exists. Other Tudor panelling sprouts carved female figures, one of which is supposed to be of Elizabeth I. Their arms are articulated, and during the Civil War they were said to be raised or lowered at dinner parties to indicate whether there were sympathisers of the opposite side present. Edmund Prideaux remodelled the room in the 18th century, and much of the panelling dates from this time. Restored after a fire in the 1890s, the room still retains its function as a dining room. The dining chairs are by Augustus Pugin, architect of the House of Commons and leader of the Gothic revival. The picture over the fireplace is of Nicholas Prideaux by Marcus Geerhearts the Younger, and is similar to his contemporary portrait of Sir Francis Drake. The ruff collar was added when Nicholas was knighted.

archaeological remains, including stone coffins and an arch and cross of the Cornish tradition, possibly from the 9th century. They may have come from an ancient chapel or hermitage dedicated to St Sampson, which was demolished in 1796 when Edmund's son Humphrey remodelled the gardens in the style of Capability Brown.

In the 1870s an ornate sunken garden was added at the northern end of the grounds, overlaying Victorian fashion on a Georgian design. The focal point was a quatrefoil pond with a fountain, and terraces led up to a conservatory or orangery (33579). The gardens fell into disuse during the First World War, and the conservatory was later demolished. Throughout the 1990s the gardens have been restored with assistance of the Cornwall Gardens Trust.

Right: **Prideaux Place, the Conservatory 1894** 33579

Below: **Prideaux Place, the Quarry Cliffs 1894** 33578
The quarry and pond lie beyond the grounds to the south of the house, and are now overgrown.

A
s is the nature of Cornish fishing towns, Padstow is a hotch-potch of alleys, private yards and quays.

There are many slate-hung and colour-washed houses in Church Street and on the Strand, which give the town character. Some of the old grey Cornish slates have been replaced with imported or artificial slates, whilst others have been painted over, and some of the stonework has been rendered. There is now a fashion to remove the render and restore the stonework. Formerly many of the streets were cobbled. Padstow had many private yards, and few remain as unspoilt as Grove Place (69705, opposite). It was built as cheap housing for working people, and it has the appearance of tied cottages for employees of the same business, such as a shipowner's. In the 1881 census there were 40 people living there in 11 houses. These included three ships' carpenters, a ship's smith, a mason and a bootmaker.

The town had a market each Saturday, and a fair for cattle and horses on the first Tuesday in May. The fair was granted by a charter of Elizabeth I at the same time as the town was made a borough. The markets remained until just after the First World War. A guide of 1895 stated that the town had two chief inns (the Commercial and St Petroc's), a custom house, a coastguard station, a church and dissenting chapels. There were two mills in the town producing flour and cattle feed, and grain was stored in warehouses on the quay.

D H Lawrence and his wife Frieda stayed at Padstow during 1915 and 1916. They were planning to head for Florida to found a literary colony, but they chose to stay in Cornwall and live at Zennor. He wrote: 'The wind blows very hard, the sea all comes up the cliffs in smoke. The sea rages under the black rocks, and the western sky is iridescent at evening'. They were disliked for ignoring blackout regulations.

In Lanadwell Street, Harriet Burt's grocery is largely unchanged today (74882, page 42, right).

Grove Place
1920 69705

Market Place 1906 56268

The Quintrells were an old local family whose stationers' and printers' shop (on the right) continued until the 1960s. Opposite is Williams' newsagents. At the end of the street, with blinds over the window, is Hawkins' butchers' shop and Sleeman's ironmongers'. Apart from the traffic, the scene has changed little.

The shop was taken over by her cousin, M J Buckingham, and passed to his son. Now it sells items for interior design. On the left of 74882 is Tonkin's shoe shop. The proprietor, Edgar Tonkin, was a keen local historian, and he recorded the Padstow carols and May Day songs. Just off the street a cinema had just been built. It is still there, remarkably surviving the demise of many other small town cinemas.

The South Western Hotel, later the Hotel Metropole (47716, 69704, 74901, pages 44-47), was built for the Cory family in 1898 at a cost of £12,000. They founded the Cory Shipping Company, which operated from Cardiff. It is not clear whether it was intended as their private residence, but by 1900 it was the South Western Hotel, named after the London and South Western Railway. Picture 47716 (pages 44-45) shows Station Road, to the right of which is the Bluff. In 69704 (pages 46-47) the Bluff has gone, used to extend the quayside.

By 1915 the South Western had become the Hotel Metropole. One can see how Padstow had become more prosperous after the arrival of the railway, with extensive gardens for new villas along Dennis Road (69709, page 48). The Prince of Wales, later Edward VIII, stayed at the Metropole in the 1920s. In 1935 the hotel was taken over by the Trust House group, now part of Trust House Forte's Heritage Hotels chain. It has fifty en suite rooms.

Lanadwell Street 1923 74882

**Marble Arch,
Church Street
1906** 56270

This is a house known as Marble Arch Cottage. Steps run up through the arch, leading to a passageway which connects with the High Street. The building is still recognisable, but the creeper has gone.

H. G. BURT,

Tea, Provision & Flour Dealer, Padstow.

Licensed to sell Tobacco
& Patent Medicines,

Shipping supplied.
....
Families waited on daily for
Orders.

ESTABLISHED 1858.

PETER TONKIN

Boot, Shoe & Legging Manufacturer, PADSTOW.
....
A Large assortment of High Grade Footwear

THE

CINEDROMES,

WADEBRIDGE — and — PADSTOW.

Nightly at 8-0.

Equipped with the latest
ALL-BRITISH
TALKIE APPARATUS.

South Western Hotel 1901 47716

PADSTOW, North Cornwall.

SOUTH WESTERN HOTEL.

FIRST-CLASS FAMILY HOTEL.   Handsomely furnished.
Very commodious.   Ideal Summer and Winter Residence.

**SPACIOUS COFFEE, READING, BILLIARD, SMOKING, AND
LADIES' DRAWING ROOMS.**

Excellent Boating, Fishing, Golfing.   Terms moderate.
Tariff on application to Miss KATE POLSUE, Manageress.

THE METROPOLE
HOTEL

A first-class Hotel in pleasant gardens.
Large new dining room with windows
facing the Estuary.   Central heating in
public rooms.   Open throughout the year.

Telephone: Padstow 7

A   TRUST   HOUSE   HOTEL

Above: **Hotel
Metropole 1923**
74901

Right: **Hotel
Metropole 1920**
69704

Above **Dennis Road 1920** 69709

Dennis Road was originally one of the town's ropewalks, where rope was made for sailing ships. The road was developed with Victorian terraced housing, but at the date of this photograph it was still little more than a country lane overlooking fields. Today the road is wider, and there is housing all around.

Right: **Trethillick Lane 1920** 69706

This was, and still is, a pleasant walk to a little hamlet, and it was popular with Victorian visitors and courting couples. It starts here at the entrance to Prideaux Place, which now has iron gates. The drive to the house was created during 18th-century landscaping.

The creek, around which Padstow grew, gradually silted up, and Middle Street now stands where the original harbour was.

The first harbour was made in Tudor times, when Sir Walter Raleigh was Warden of the Cornish Stannaries, which were courts administering special laws for tin miners, and here he collected legal dues from the tin mines. He was given the job so that he could strengthen the defences of the area against possible invasion by the Spanish, who were inciting the Irish to rebel. A Spanish attack was repulsed in 1591.

In 1895 there were a hundred vessels registered to Padstow. Most were small and averaged 84 tons. Five hundred vessels a year from outside would come and go, carrying 28,000 tons of cargo. Page, writing in 1897, said: 'The trade is not very extensive, the exports consisting of fish, slate and agricultural produce, the imports chiefly of coal'. The coal was used at a gasworks in town, and was soon to be brought by train. Before the railway came there was much reliance on herrings and pilchards, which could be preserved by salting and smoking. Afterwards an ice and packing factory for fresh fish was set up on the North Quay (P1054, page 54). Many of the quay buildings were sail lofts, chandlers and boat stores. Nowadays they are mainly shops, cafés and flats.

Beyond the north arm of the quay, the new Riverside Café and ballroom occupies the site of

The Harbour 1888 21213

The Harbour
1888 21214

Right: **The Harbour 1901** 47715

The vessel in the foreground is the ketch 'Frances', owned by Captain Moore and later sunk by a German submarine. Behind are schooners typical of those built in Padstow. On the skyline is the South Western Hotel, and below it is Sir Walter Raleigh's Court House, standing behind iron railings.

Below Left: **The Harbour 1901** 47714

Below Right: **The Harbour 1901** 47712

Moored at the old harbour wall are two schooners. Some of these were armed with canon during the First World War. Part of the harbour wall on which they are berthed was built in 1536; it is the oldest surviving part of the harbour. Behind is Hawkens coal store, which later became a fishing store. To its right is the Seamen's Room, belonging to the Royal National Mission to Deep Sea Fishermen.

the former ice factory (P1054, page 54). Before that it was the site of Padstow's electric light works, which was put out of business by the National Grid. Before that it was the Lower Yard, where many timber ships were built. The café itself has now been demolished and replaced by flats and a gift shop. The shelter to its left is still there, and another has been built on the site of the shed. A plaque on the shelter commemorates Claude Berry (1895-1976), 'writer, broadcaster and devoted son of Padstow'. He wrote much about the town, as did the journalist Stephan Fuller, who is also commemorated.

The railway station was built on a former shipyard and on land reclaimed from the estuary. Work on the south jetty and sidings began in 1911 and finished the following year. There was a turntable, and a siding served a fish shed. Fish were landed straight into the shed, boxed or barrelled, and put on trains which pulled in under a wooden canopy. Fish carried by rail increased from 24 tons in 1900 to 3,074 tons in 1911. Special Billingsgate fish trains were run in the mid afternoon, and extra trains were laid on during the peak season from January to March. Even old railway coaches were adapted for the freight. East coast drifters and trawlers made Padstow their home for winter fishing. They called its rich fishing grounds 'Klondike'. They would alternate between Padstow and Swansea, where they would take on coal. For a while Padstow was really bustling. However, in the First World War many trawlers, up to thirteen in one day, were sunk by German submarines, and the east coast fleet left.

On the South Quay was a row of warehouses (P1005, page 56). On the far left is that of Bray and Parken, now part of the Old Custom House inn. Next to it were two inns: the Caledonia (the 'Calley') and the Commercial, now the Harbour Inn. Beyond that is another Bray and Parken warehouse, which took over Henwood's warehouse next door. The sign on the latter is still just visible. The garage has now been demolished, opening up one side of the Drang, a local word for a narrow street or alley. The other side of the the Drang is a slated building which was formerly a candle house, now the Lobster Pot shop.

View P1078 shows a new car park on the old part of North Quay, and in the foreground, on the South Quay, another car park has been built on land reclaimed from the sea. Behind the parked cars is the Old Custom House, now joined to old warehouses as the Custom House inn. A Custom House was set up in Padstow in the mid 17th century to counteract the smuggling that was rife in the area. Outside the house was a pair of davits to lower the preventative cutter into the sea.

Behind the warehouses shown in 74879, (pages 60-61) was another built in 1870, and replaced in 1991 by a new building called the Red Brick Building after its predecessor. It has been rebuilt to look like a warehouse, but it contains flats, the Tourist Information Centre and the headquarters of Padstow Rowing Club. On the walls are plaques to sailors and fishermen who were drowned in

Right: **The Harbour c1960** P1078

Below: **The Quay c1960** P1054

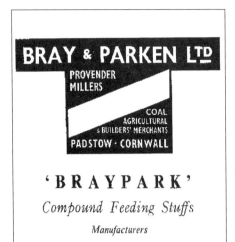

'BRAYPARK'

Compound Feeding Stuffs

Manufacturers

natural and wartime disasters.

A more ambitious project was the building of the outside south arm of the dock, completed in phases in 1915, 1928 and 1935. The last phase included the building of the north arm under a Government employment scheme during the Depression. The inner harbour is now provided with lock gates, which are opened by the Harbour Commissioners to allow boats in and out at high tide. Along with a sea wall, they form part of Padstow's Tidal Defence Scheme, completed in 1990 to prevent the flooding of the town at spring tides.

In the mid 1930s large quantities of china clay

South Quay c1960 P1005

Above: **The Quay 1935** 86672

This was taken shortly after the quays were completed, and shows Padstow as a commercial port. At the far end of the harbour we can see the dock with the fish shed and the old black smoke house for making kippers.

Below: **The Harbour c1960** P1067

The Quay
1923 74903

The Harbour 1923 74879

In the centre of the picture are warehouses, including F & J Martyn's timber warehouse. The roof to the right was part of a timber workshop supplying local shipyards. Outside was a sawpit. Recently it became the Shipwright's Inn.

were landed here for shipment, instead of at Fowey. There was a two-ton crane, and also a two-storey block of fish merchant's offices. Much rail transport of fish was lost after an enginemen's strike in 1955. Now much of the shellfish caught locally goes by lorry to Spain. The ice factory burned down in 1950, resulting in the loss of most of the trawling fleet. The fish shed was converted to the Museum of Shipwrecks. After the closure of the railway in 1967, the station building was converted to offices for Customs and Excise and Padstow Town Council. The old platform provides parking for bicycles using the Camel trail.

Recent provision of ice and diesel has attracted fishing boats back to Padstow, particularly for shellfish. The National Lobster Hatchery, on the quay, was constructed to replenish stocks of shellfish and as an educational facility. Today the harbour can accommodate vessels of up to 2000 tons; in recent years cargoes have included fertilisers, grain, animal feeds, coal and timber. Sand is dredged from the estuary and lifted by crane onto

Right: **North Quay c1960** P1003
Along the quayside there is evidence of Padstow becoming run down, owing to the dwindling of the fishing industry. The dilapidated building to the left was previously the Harbour Café, and later Ellery's Sunnyside Café; it is now an estate agents'. To the right of it is the Harbour View Private Hotel, now holiday flats, and next to the former office of timber merchants F & J Martyn in what was originally sail lofts. Beyond is the Abbey House, and to its right are the electricity offices, now the Quayside Café.

Below Left: **The Harbour c1960** P1038

Below Right: **North Quay c1960** P1069

the quay. Because of its high lime content from shells, it is used as an agricultural fertiliser.

By the 1960s, much fishing was part-time or for pleasure. In P1038 (page 62) we can see some of the inshore fishing boats in the inner harbour. In the foreground is the 'Girl Maureen', belonging to Tommy Morrisey. Before that it was the 'Kingfisher' and before that the 'Docea Chapman', a pulling (rowing) lifeboat. Originating as the Withernsea lifeboat before the First World War, it became Padstow's second lifeboat in 1938. It is now restored as a lifeboat in the Exmoor National Park Visitor Centre at Lynmouth.

The Quay at Low Tide c1960 P1032

In the centre of the picture is the Cory Shelter, built in 1938 in memory of Sir Herbert Cory, a member of the shipping family who built what is now the Metropole Hotel. The long seat beside the shelter, on the corner of North Quay, was known as the 'Long Lugger'. It was a traditional meeting and gossiping place used by older locals, who were known as 'Padstow's Parliament'.

The Cliff Path to the Coastguard Station 1931 84331

The Camel estuary is the only safe haven on a long stretch of coast. Famous voyagers sheltered there: Sir John Hawkins on his return from the West Indies, Sir Martin Frobisher after his quest for the north-west passage to China, and Sir Walter Raleigh.

The river is said to take its name from the Cornish 'Cam Alan' or 'Camheyle', meaning crooked river. The Doom Bar partly blocks its mouth. A legend surrounding it tells of Jan Tregeagle, a real live character renowned for his ruthlessness. He is said to have shot a fairy carrying a bag of sand, which she dropped to form the bar. On his death, the story is that he was made to undertake impossible tasks to save his soul from the Devil. One task was to plait a rope of sand, and

some say the bar was a result of his fruitless attempts. Another theory is that it is named because of its many shipwrecks. Yet another is that it is a corruption of Dune Bar, from the sand dunes nearby.

Padstow harbour is sheltered, but in 150 years over 300 vessels were wrecked or stranded whilst approaching it. In 1829 the Padstow Harbour Association for the Preservation of Life and Property from Shipwreck was founded by Squire Charles Prideaux-Brune. This was mainly to assist ships in navigating the narrow channel through the bar near Stepper Point. (This channel has since moved to the far side of the estuary). When they had rounded the Point, ships were often becalmed in its lee or thrown backwards by

The War Memorial 1923 74885

The memorial was unveiled by a Mrs Bate in 1922. Armistice Day parades had previously congregated at the cemetery. Names were added to the far side after the Second World War. It was across the estuary that Laurence Binyon wrote the poem 'For the Fallen' that is often read at Remembrance Day. The memorial stands at the end of a park with many memorial seats for local people, and it is a peaceful place to sit and admire the views of the estuary.

eddies. The Association erected three capstans for winching ships through the channel. A guide of 1895 states: 'A capstan is on Stepper Point, at the mouth of the estuary, 27 feet above sea level; and on the arrival of a vessel in the offing during a prevalence of adverse winds, a hawser is conveyed from the capstan by a pilot boat to the vessel to aid its passage over the bar'. Steam tugs were also used to tow sailing ships over the bar.

Another plan of the Association was to blast a cutting across Stepper Point so that ships could hold the wind blowing through it. The ambitious scheme was started but not finished, although quarrying on the Point later completed the gap - quarrying for road stone continued until the 1960s. The stone was loaded into boats from a quay at the foot of the cliff. There is now little sign of the industry, apart from the quarry itself. A navigation light stands at the end of the quarry to mark the entrance to the estuary. Originally, a local from Hawkers Cove set out every evening to light the oil lamp. The Association erected a daymark on the Point prior to the building of Trevose lighthouse. The forty-foot tower, originally designed to hold a fire beacon, still stands as a navigation aid.

From Chapel Stile (47720, below) one can see

Church Chapel Stile 1901 47720

Known simply as 'Stile', this is on St Saviour's Point. It is said that St Petroc founded ten ancient chapels in the monastic manor of Padstow. Five were in the town: St Samson's, St Wetheny's, St Leonard's, St Saviour's and the Blessed Virgin Mary. Others were St Samson's at Hawkers Cove, St Saviery's at Trethillick, St Constantine's at Trevone, St Cadoc's at Harlyn and St Michael's at Four Turnings. Old pictures show what are supposed to have been the ruins of St Saviour's below the stile. Here a hermit was said to have kept a beacon to guide sailors to the harbour.

the estuary from Stepper and Pentire Points back to Padstow, the tidal swimming pool and Ship my Pumps Point. A story goes that the latter is named thus because it is where boats would start pumping out their bilges when just clear of the harbour. Another theory is that it is named after small blowholes in the rocks known as Chidley Pumps. Across the estuary are other places with unusual names, such as Sinkininney, Pityme and Gentle Jane. With such a fine view, it is no wonder that a battery was situated at nearby Gun Point to protect the harbour. There were guns there from the time of Elizabeth I, and the remains of a 19th-century gun emplacement can still be seen, together with remains from the Second World War.

A local saying goes: 'From Padstow Point to Lundy Light is a watery grave by day or night'. In 1790 Padstow had a special gig for life saving, making it one of the oldest lifeboat stations in Britain. Its first lifeboat proper was built in 1827, and the RNLI took over in 1856. Padstow lifeboats had their share of success and disaster. The lifeboat 'Albert Edward' suffered tragedy in 1867 when five of the crew were drowned going to the rescue of an American schooner on the Doom Bar. In 1900 the steam lifeboat 'James Stephens' capsized; eight of the crew were lost, plus three fishermen and a rowing lifeboat, the 'Arab'. Rowing lifeboats were kept as second boats, and were towed to rescues by steam tugs.

Although originally based in Padstow, the

The Lifeboat Station 1931 84332

The old lifeboat station is in Hawkers Cove, which is reputedly named after medieval falconers from the monastery. The number one lifeboat house and its equipment store are now private houses, but the number two lifeboat house, in service until 1968, is disused. Here are the houses built for the Trinity House gig pilots, who set out from the cove to guide ships into the estuary. Newer houses were built for the coastguards, whose role was to prevent smuggling as well as to watch for ships in distress. During the First World War the Royal Flying Corps had an airfield nearby, and kept six motor launches in the cove to chase German submarines.

lifeboat was later kept at Hawkers Cove (84332, opposite) inside the estuary. With the silting up of the estuary, the boats were often pulled by horses and carriage to the beach nearest to the vessel in danger. From 1961 an offshore lifeboat was kept in the estuary to be ready at all times, but it could not always cross the bar at low tide. In 1967 the station was relocated to the open coast at Mother Ivey's Bay near Trevose Head, three miles from the town, and a Land Rover was kept at Padstow to carry the crew to the boathouse. The boathouse was opened by the Duke of Kent, who the same day named the new lifeboat the 'James and Catherine MacFarlane'. It was the gift of the biscuit magnate Robert MacFarlane, and it is now a Land's End tourist attraction.

There was once a ferry between Wadebridge and Padstow, a journey which can now only be made in a small boat at high tide. It seems to have run during the 19th century until it was made redundant by the coming of the railway. It carried a little freight as well as passengers, and cut the road journey by three miles.

The Padstow to Rock ferry service has been operating at least since the Duchy of Cornwall was created in 1337, and was known as the Duchy Ferry. Tenants rented the ferry from the Manor of Penmayne on the Rock side of the river. Little is known of its history except that its rent rose sharply during the 19th century, reflecting the increased revenue from tourists. Since then the rights have been leased by the Duchy to Padstow Harbour Commissioners.

A horse and wagon boat operated until the 1890s, when it was replaced by a rowing boat with a lugsail. Page wrote: 'The short cruise of twenty minutes or so is pleasant enough - that is in fine weather. When, however, a stiff breeze is blowing up or down the estuary matters are

The Lifeboat 1931 84334

The 'Sunbeam' 1888
21217

The 'Sunbeam' was a three-masted topsail schooner built in 1874 for Lord Brassey. Son of railway pioneer Thomas Brassey, he was a naval administrator and Civil Lord of the Admiralty. He sailed around the world in the 'Sunbeam' between 1876 and 1877, taking his family with him in grand style. An account of the voyage, written by Lady Brassey, became a classic of sailing literature, making the 'Sunbeam' famous. She also took part in a trans-Atlantic race. Lord Brassey, then Earl Brassey, died in 1918; after several changes of ownership, the 'Sunbeam' was broken up in 1930.

rather different: as likely or not you will get a wet coat. Indeed the passage at times is really dangerous: only last winter (1894) this very boat in which we are now sitting capsized in a squall and both the ferrymen drowned'. In 1906 the ferry was again capsized in a squall, and the ferryman, Hodge Helbren, was drowned. The sailing boat was replaced by a motor boat in 1913, which was run by Joss Rawe and his son Will. William England worked the ferry when Will was away at war, and held on to the lease afterwards. He worked the last sailing ferries. There was a service every hour in winter, and a continuous service in the summer. The following owner, Stephen Brabyn, worked the ferry for 14 years with three motor boats. The toll was 3d, and regular passengers included builders, golfers and caddies for the course at St Enodoc. After that Brabyn's nephew, Bill Lindsey, took over until 1966, using boats mostly built in his own shipyard (P1068, page 74).

J L W Page, writing in 1897, described Rock as 'a line of cottages with a villa or two'. According to John Betjeman, it had 'an inn, a Georgian house or two, a Victorian terrace, tamarisks, elms, a wharf

Right: **St George's Well 1901** 47721

St George's Cove is named after St George's holy well. According to legend, St George's horse struck a rock here with its hoof and a spring issued forth, but there is no spring now. There was once a brick kiln and a quarry here.

Below: **St George's Well 1923** 74888

The beach became a favourite picnic place for the gentry, including the Prideaux-Brunes. An old cottage, just seen behind the bushes to the right, overlooked the beach until the 1980s. It was used by the family for changing and for servants to prepare their picnics.

DEAD SLOW

Above: **The Ferry and the Harbour Entrance c1960** P1068

The last boatman to have a sub-lease from the Harbour Commissioners was John England, grandson of William. The Commissioners have operated the ferry themselves since 1973. Their boats were unnamed, and were fitted with landing steps, as the landing at Rock kept being destroyed by the shifting sands. The ferry uses the harbour wall at Padstow except at low tide, when a landing further downstream is used. As the tide drops, the ferry has to go further to navigate Town Bar, and at lowest tide it has to find deep water off St Saviour's Point.

Left: **St George's Well 1931** 84329
By the 1930s, the beach had become popular with all sorts of holidaymakers.

Below: **Rock from Padstow Harbour c1960** P1036

and a quay and many detached villas, a few by architects'. A notable building was the Rock Hotel, popular with golfers, sailors and drinkers, and demolished in 1976. Escaping demolition at the same time was the old warehouse, which was renovated by the Rock Sailing Club. Originally a store for coal and grain, it never seems to have been a Customs House, as it is now called. Rock still has boatyards, which specialise in smaller boats such as sailing dinghies and traditional Cornish cobles.

Golfing at Rock is said to have been started by a group of undergraduates playing on the dunes in 1888. A club was started in 1891, and a famous golfer, James Braid, laid out a full 18-hole course in 1907. A 9-hole course was added in 1967. The course is of championship standard, and it has been patronised by royalty on several occasions.

Beside the estuary, above Padstow, were slate quarries. They are now derelict and flooded, with terraces and spoil heaps and the remains of engine houses and landing stages where coasters came to load up the slate. The purplish-grey slate was used for flagstones, roofing tiles, chimney pieces and water tanks. At the end of the 17th century, over a million slates a year were being exported from there. A sheltered inlet runs up to Little Petherick, where there is an old quay, a church dedicated to St Petroc and a stretch of road said to be haunted by a monk. Further upstream, much of the side of the estuary is wooded and remarkably unspoilt.

The Atlantic Coast Express was a favourite journey for Sir John Betjeman. He wrote: 'The fireman checks his fire, trickles a few in across the back and takes his seat to watch the road and the scenery. A man painting a boat at Oldtown Cove turns and waves as the train passes on the causeway behind him. Speed is reduced to 15 mph for Little Petherick creek bridge, which consists of three 150ft trusses set on a curve (56273, above), the train passes through a last rock cutting and we coast into Padstow station'.

Right: **The Railway Bridge 1906**
56273

The broad creek to Little Petherick was the major challenge in constructing the branch line. A bridge of three 130ft spans was built at the end of an embankment running into the creek. The legs were 8ft diameter cylinders which were sunk 53ft through the estuary mud to rock, and filled with concrete. The bridge was built on a 10-chain curve, necessitating a speed limit for trains.

Right: **The View across the Camel from Rock c1960**
P1048

There is a tradition that St Petroc originally landed near Rock, where he met a group of reapers who taunted him to demonstrate his holiness. He struck a rock with his staff, and a spring issued from it. However, Rock is probably named after Black Rock, a former estuary landmark. Nowadays the area is sandy, and dunes run to Daymer Bay. Two churches - St Enodoc (the burial place of Sir John Betjeman) and St Michael - have been dug out from the constantly shifting sands.

Right: **Looking Up River 1906** 56272

Below: **The View from the Jubilee Tower 1906** 56271

The 56ft monument on Dennis Hill was built to mark the Diamond Jubilee of Queen Victoria in 1897. A time capsule was placed underneath it containing newspapers and coins of the day. There are panoramic views of the whole Camel estuary. This view looks down on Dennis Creek, where there was once a shipyard. We can see the railway line - it was here that the railway company planned to build sidings for a proposed extension to Newquay.

CS Ward, the author who did not think Padstow was worth visiting for its own sake, was more complimentary about the estuary and coast beyond. Writing in 1895, he said of Padstow: '... but those fond of a fine coast will find it a convenient resting-place for the night'. He recommended that visitors hired a boatman from Hawkers Cove to take them down the coast to see the seals and the great gullies beyond Stepper Point.

Harlyn Bay (69711, pages 80-81) was the site of an important archaeological find, discovered in 1900 while the foundations for a house were being dug. Excavations have since revealed Bronze Age burial grounds dating from about 600BC. Two gold crescent-shaped ornaments known as 'lunulae', probably dating from 1500BC, were found nearby. When the house at Harlyn was eventually built, a small local museum was attached to display some pieces. The Harlyn Inn now stands on the site, and

most of the finds are in the county museum at Truro. The old house of Harlyn is inland. Parts of it are over five hundred years old, and it has an interesting dovecote.

In Elizabethan times a local buccaneer, John Pearce, is said to have landed his Spanish treasure at Harlyn Bay (69711, pages 80-81). The bay was the scene of a skirmish with the Spanish in 1595. Padstow was well defended on the estuary side: when the Spanish, under Captain Pedro de Amazola, tried to land their galliasses at Harlyn and attack overland, they were spotted and repulsed by local militia.

In the sand dunes on Trevose golf course are a holy well and the ruins of Constantine's Church, which may be linked with Constantine, an ancient Cornish king and martyr. His well was said to have miraculous powers, and pilgrims bathed their feet there. The chapel was rebuilt about 1390, and continued in use until the 16th century, when it

Cliffs at Porth Missen c1880
13211a

Porth Missen, near Trevone, is also known as Permizen, a name that may mean a port with oak woods. There are no woods now. The cliffs are 200ft high, and there is magnificent cliff scenery, with alternating strata of slate and quartz exposed at Marble Cliffs, quartz-seamed rocks at Permizen Point, the great rock split at Tregudda Gorge, two natural arches at Porthmissen Bridge and Round Hole, and a great blowhole in the middle of a field.

became waterlogged and partly engulfed by sand. The well was rediscovered in 1911.

The coastline west of Padstow was noted for smuggling and wrecking in the 18th century. This was linked with poverty. Wages were poor, especially in the mines, work was hard, and life expectancy was short. Much local food produce was exported to fetch higher prices, and there were food shortages. High corn prices led to riots in the 18th and 19th centuries. Miners seized a corn ship in Padstow, and on Stepper Point is Butter Hole, reputedly named after a ship full of butter which was wrecked there. Pepper Hole may be named after the wreck of a spice ship. Some of the fraud, smuggling and wrecking was backed by the wealthy, and even clergy were involved. The preaching of Methodism, however, tried to counteract the lawlessness.

All along the coast are the remains of copper mines and Second World War look-outs and fortifications. The mines were both deep mines and surface workings. They had long lives of boom and bust, eventually ceasing in the late 19th century.

Communal seine netting took place from the beaches in April and May, when mullet was a common catch, along with the usual pilchards. There are old fish cellars at the back of Harlyn beach where the catch was salted and barrelled. Today, the beach is backed by hotels, holiday flats, and a camping and caravan site, plus a pub and shop. The huge wide crescent of a beach seems to absorb any number of visitors.

Trevose Head is named after the Cornish word 'fos', which means an embankment, suggesting that there was once a cliff fort here. It commands a view from Hartland Point to near Lands End. The 75ft-high lighthouse (33573a, pages 82-83) was built in 1847, and it flashes a red light. It had two lights, one at the top and one at the base of the tower, and it was one of the last in Britain to be

Above Left: **Porthcothan Bay 1894** 33580a

Porthcothan was described in a guide book of the time as: 'a knot of cottages at the head of a cove, the sands of which are wet with the waters of a stream coming down the wild half-wooded valley beyond'. In the valley side was a tunnel, supposedly a thousand yards long, associated with smuggling. At the time the valley was mostly cultivated, now it is well-wooded. The beach was mined during the First World War, and dunes grew up around the safety fencing. This is a real gem of a beach sheltered by cliffs, some of which are protected by the National Trust.

Below Left: **Harlyn Bay 1920** 69711

The wreck on the beach was that of the 'Industry'. The name of this bay means 'beside the pool'.

**Trevose Head
Lighthouse
1894** 33573a

run on paraffin. It is open to the public when convenient. Out at sea, the projecting fingers of the Quies Rocks are a reminder of the need for the lighthouse and the nearby Coastguard lookout.

The coastline is impressive, but as one guide book says, for those who have memories of happy childhoods spent on the beaches, 'they are still there, of course, but many of the approaches and the skylines seem to be dominated now by caravan parks and bungalows'.

The long, narrow bay at Treyarnon is at an angle to the waves sweeping in from the Atlantic, and provides some of the best surfing around. The cliffs and headlands, however, provide shelter, and there is a natural tidal pool for children to swim in. The bay is now backed by a large car park, hotels, a caravan and camping site and a Youth Hostel. It looks out to the rocky Trethias Island, a nature reserve.

Above: **Treyarnon Bay 1936** 87605

Left: **Treyarnon Bay c1960** P1082

Index

Frith Book Co Titles

www.francisfrith.co.uk

The Frith Book Company publishes over 100 new titles each year. A selection of those currently available are listed below. For latest catalogue please contact Frith Book Co.

Town Books 96 pages, approx 100 photos. County and Themed Books 128 pages, approx 150 photos (unless specified). All titles hardback laminated case and jacket except those indicated pb (paperback)

Amersham, Chesham & Rickmansworth (pb)			Derby (pb)	1-85937-367-4	£9.99
	1-85937-340-2	£9.99	Derbyshire (pb)	1-85937-196-5	£9.99
Ancient Monuments & Stone Circles	1-85937-143-4	£17.99	Devon (pb)	1-85937-297-x	£9.99
Aylesbury (pb)	1-85937-227-9	£9.99	Dorset (pb)	1-85937-269-4	£9.99
Bakewell	1-85937-113-2	£12.99	Dorset Churches	1-85937-172-8	£17.99
Barnstaple (pb)	1-85937-300-3	£9.99	Dorset Coast (pb)	1-85937-299-6	£9.99
Bath (pb)	1-85937419-0	£9.99	Dorset Living Memories	1-85937-210-4	£14.99
Bedford (pb)	1-85937-205-8	£9.99	Down the Severn	1-85937-118-3	£14.99
Berkshire (pb)	1-85937-191-4	£9.99	Down the Thames (pb)	1-85937-278-3	£9.99
Berkshire Churches	1-85937-170-1	£17.99	Down the Trent	1-85937-311-9	£14.99
Blackpool (pb)	1-85937-382-8	£9.99	Dublin (pb)	1-85937-231-7	£9.99
Bognor Regis (pb)	1-85937-431-x	£9.99	East Anglia (pb)	1-85937-265-1	£9.99
Bournemouth	1-85937-067-5	£12.99	East London	1-85937-080-2	£14.99
Bradford (pb)	1-85937-204-x	£9.99	East Sussex	1-85937-130-2	£14.99
Brighton & Hove(pb)	1-85937-192-2	£8.99	Eastbourne	1-85937-061-6	£12.99
Bristol (pb)	1-85937-264-3	£9.99	Edinburgh (pb)	1-85937-193-0	£8.99
British Life A Century Ago (pb)	1-85937-213-9	£9.99	England in the 1880s	1-85937-331-3	£17.99
Buckinghamshire (pb)	1-85937-200-7	£9.99	English Castles (pb)	1-85937-434-4	£9.99
Camberley (pb)	1-85937-222-8	£9.99	English Country Houses	1-85937-161-2	£17.99
Cambridge (pb)	1-85937-422-0	£9.99	Essex (pb)	1-85937-270-8	£9.99
Cambridgeshire (pb)	1-85937-420-4	£9.99	Exeter	1-85937-126-4	£12.99
Canals & Waterways (pb)	1-85937-291-0	£9.99	Exmoor	1-85937-132-9	£14.99
Canterbury Cathedral (pb)	1-85937-179-5	£9.99	Falmouth	1-85937-066-7	£12.99
Cardiff (pb)	1-85937-093-4	£9.99	Folkestone (pb)	1-85937-124-8	£9.99
Carmarthenshire	1-85937-216-3	£14.99	Glasgow (pb)	1-85937-190-6	£9.99
Chelmsford (pb)	1-85937-310-0	£9.99	Gloucestershire	1-85937-102-7	£14.99
Cheltenham (pb)	1-85937-095-0	£9.99	Great Yarmouth (pb)	1-85937-426-3	£9.99
Cheshire (pb)	1-85937-271-6	£9.99	Greater Manchester (pb)	1-85937-266-x	£9.99
Chester	1-85937-090-x	£12.99	Guildford (pb)	1-85937-410-7	£9.99
Chesterfield	1-85937-378-x	£9.99	Hampshire (pb)	1-85937-279-1	£9.99
Chichester (pb)	1-85937-228-7	£9.99	Hampshire Churches (pb)	1-85937-207-4	£9.99
Colchester (pb)	1-85937-188-4	£8.99	Harrogate	1-85937-423-9	£9.99
Cornish Coast	1-85937-163-9	£14.99	Hastings & Bexhill (pb)	1-85937-131-0	£9.99
Cornwall (pb)	1-85937-229-5	£9.99	Heart of Lancashire (pb)	1-85937-197-3	£9.99
Cornwall Living Memories	1-85937-248-1	£14.99	Helston (pb)	1-85937-214-7	£9.99
Cotswolds (pb)	1-85937-230-9	£9.99	Hereford (pb)	1-85937-175-2	£9.99
Cotswolds Living Memories	1-85937-255-4	£14.99	Herefordshire	1-85937-174-4	£14.99
County Durham	1-85937-123-x	£14.99	Hertfordshire (pb)	1-85937-247-3	£9.99
Croydon Living Memories	1-85937-162-0	£9.99	Horsham (pb)	1-85937-432-8	£9.99
Cumbria	1-85937-101-9	£14.99	Humberside	1-85937-215-5	£14.99
Dartmoor	1-85937-145-0	£14.99	Hythe, Romney Marsh & Ashford	1-85937-256-2	£9.99

Available from your local bookshop or from the publisher

Frith Book Co Titles (continued)

Ipswich (pb)	1-85937-424-7	£9.99	St Ives (pb)	1-85937415-8	£9.99
Ireland (pb)	1-85937-181-7	£9.99	Scotland (pb)	1-85937-182-5	£9.99
Isle of Man (pb)	1-85937-268-6	£9.99	Scottish Castles (pb)	1-85937-323-2	£9.99
Isles of Scilly	1-85937-136-1	£14.99	Sevenoaks & Tunbridge	1-85937-057-8	£12.99
Isle of Wight (pb)	1-85937-429-8	£9.99	Sheffield, South Yorks (pb)	1-85937-267-8	£9.99
Isle of Wight Living Memories	1-85937-304-6	£14.99	Shrewsbury (pb)	1-85937-325-9	£9.99
Kent (pb)	1-85937-189-2	£9.99	Shropshire (pb)	1-85937-326-7	£9.99
Kent Living Memories	1-85937-125-6	£14.99	Somerset	1-85937-153-1	£14.99
Lake District (pb)	1-85937-275-9	£9.99	South Devon Coast	1-85937-107-8	£14.99
Lancaster, Morecambe & Heysham (pb)	1-85937-233-3	£9.99	South Devon Living Memories	1-85937-168-x	£14.99
Leeds (pb)	1-85937-202-3	£9.99	South Hams	1-85937-220-1	£14.99
Leicester	1-85937-073-x	£12.99	Southampton (pb)	1-85937-427-1	£9.99
Leicestershire (pb)	1-85937-185-x	£9.99	Southport (pb)	1-85937-425-5	£9.99
Lincolnshire (pb)	1-85937-433-6	£9.99	Staffordshire	1-85937-047-0	£12.99
Liverpool & Merseyside (pb)	1-85937-234-1	£9.99	Stratford upon Avon	1-85937-098-5	£12.99
London (pb)	1-85937-183-3	£9.99	Suffolk (pb)	1-85937-221-x	£9.99
Ludlow (pb)	1-85937-176-0	£9.99	Suffolk Coast	1-85937-259-7	£14.99
Luton (pb)	1-85937-235-x	£9.99	Surrey (pb)	1-85937-240-6	£9.99
Maidstone	1-85937-056-x	£14.99	Sussex (pb)	1-85937-184-1	£9.99
Manchester (pb)	1-85937-198-1	£9.99	Swansea (pb)	1-85937-167-1	£9.99
Middlesex	1-85937-158-2	£14.99	Tees Valley & Cleveland	1-85937-211-2	£14.99
New Forest	1-85937-128-0	£14.99	Thanet (pb)	1-85937-116-7	£9.99
Newark (pb)	1-85937-366-6	£9.99	Tiverton (pb)	1-85937-178-7	£9.99
Newport, Wales (pb)	1-85937-258-9	£9.99	Torbay	1-85937-063-2	£12.99
Newquay (pb)	1-85937-421-2	£9.99	Truro	1-85937-147-7	£12.99
Norfolk (pb)	1-85937-195-7	£9.99	Victorian and Edwardian Cornwall	1-85937-252-x	£14.99
Norfolk Living Memories	1-85937-217-1	£14.99	Victorian & Edwardian Devon	1-85937-253-8	£14.99
Northamptonshire	1-85937-150-7	£14.99	Victorian & Edwardian Kent	1-85937-149-3	£14.99
Northumberland Tyne & Wear (pb)	1-85937-281-3	£9.99	Vic & Ed Maritime Album	1-85937-144-2	£17.99
North Devon Coast	1-85937-146-9	£14.99	Victorian and Edwardian Sussex	1-85937-157-4	£14.99
North Devon Living Memories	1-85937-261-9	£14.99	Victorian & Edwardian Yorkshire	1-85937-154-x	£14.99
North London	1-85937-206-6	£14.99	Victorian Seaside	1-85937-159-0	£17.99
North Wales (pb)	1-85937-298-8	£9.99	Villages of Devon (pb)	1-85937-293-7	£9.99
North Yorkshire (pb)	1-85937-236-8	£9.99	Villages of Kent (pb)	1-85937-294-5	£9.99
Norwich (pb)	1-85937-194-9	£8.99	Villages of Sussex (pb)	1-85937-295-3	£9.99
Nottingham (pb)	1-85937-324-0	£9.99	Warwickshire (pb)	1-85937-203-1	£9.99
Nottinghamshire (pb)	1-85937-187-6	£9.99	Welsh Castles (pb)	1-85937-322-4	£9.99
Oxford (pb)	1-85937-411-5	£9.99	West Midlands (pb)	1-85937-289-9	£9.99
Oxfordshire (pb)	1-85937-430-1	£9.99	West Sussex	1-85937-148-5	£14.99
Peak District (pb)	1-85937-280-5	£9.99	West Yorkshire (pb)	1-85937-201-5	£9.99
Penzance	1-85937-069-1	£12.99	Weymouth (pb)	1-85937-209-0	£9.99
Peterborough (pb)	1-85937-219-8	£9.99	Wiltshire (pb)	1-85937-277-5	£9.99
Piers	1-85937-237-6	£17.99	Wiltshire Churches (pb)	1-85937-171-x	£9.99
Plymouth	1-85937-119-1	£12.99	Wiltshire Living Memories	1-85937-245-7	£14.99
Poole & Sandbanks (pb)	1-85937-251-1	£9.99	Winchester (pb)	1-85937-428-x	£9.99
Preston (pb)	1-85937-212-0	£9.99	Windmills & Watermills	1-85937-242-2	£17.99
Reading (pb)	1-85937-238-4	£9.99	Worcester (pb)	1-85937-165-5	£9.99
Romford (pb)	1-85937-319-4	£9.99	Worcestershire	1-85937-152-3	£14.99
Salisbury (pb)	1-85937-239-2	£9.99	York (pb)	1-85937-199-x	£9.99
Scarborough (pb)	1-85937-379-8	£9.99	Yorkshire (pb)	1-85937-186-8	£9.99
St Albans (pb)	1-85937-341-0	£9.99	Yorkshire Living Memories	1-85937-166-3	£14.99

See Frith books on the internet www.francisfrith.co.uk

FRITH PRODUCTS & SERVICES

Francis Frith would doubtless be pleased to know that the pioneering publishing venture he started in 1860 still continues today. A hundred and forty years later, The Francis Frith Collection continues in the same innovative tradition and is now one of the foremost publishers of vintage photographs in the world. Some of the current activities include:

Interior Decoration

Today Frith's photographs can be seen framed and as giant wall murals in thousands of pubs, restaurants, hotels, banks, retail stores and other public buildings throughout the country. In every case they enhance the unique local atmosphere of the places they depict and provide reminders of gentler days in an increasingly busy and frenetic world.

Product Promotions

Frith products are used by many major companies to promote the sales of their own products or to reinforce their own history and heritage. Frith promotions have been used by Hovis bread, Courage beers, Scots Porage Oats, Colman's mustard, Cadbury's foods, Mellow Birds coffee, Dunhill pipe tobacco, Guinness, and Bulmer's Cider.

Genealogy and Family History

As the interest in family history and roots grows world-wide, more and more people are turning to Frith's photographs of Great Britain for images of the towns, villages and streets where their ancestors lived; and, of course, photographs of the churches and chapels where their ancestors were christened, married and buried are an essential part of every genealogy tree and family album.

Frith Products

All Frith photographs are available Framed or just as Mounted Prints and Posters (size 23 x 16 inches). These may be ordered from the address below. From time to time other products - Address Books, Calendars, Table Mats, etc - are available.

The Internet

Already twenty thousand Frith photographs can be viewed and purchased on the internet through the Frith websites and a myriad of partner sites.

For more detailed information on Frith companies and products, look at these sites:

www.francisfrith.co.uk
www.francisfrith.com
(for North American visitors)

See the complete list of Frith Books at:
www.francisfrith.co.uk
This web site is regularly updated with the latest list of publications from the Frith Book Company. If you wish to buy books relating to another part of the country that your local bookshop does not stock, you may purchase on-line.

For further information, trade, or author enquiries please contact us at the address below:
The Francis Frith Collection, Frith's Barn, Teffont, Salisbury, Wiltshire, England SP3 5QP.
Tel: +44 (0)1722 716 376 Fax: +44 (0)1722 716 881 Email: sales@francisfrith.co.uk

See Frith books on the internet www.francisfrith.co.uk

TO RECEIVE YOUR FREE MOUNTED PRINT

Mounted Print
Overall size 14 x 11 inches

Cut out this Voucher and return it with your remittance for £2.25 to cover postage and handling, to UK addresses. For overseas addresses please include £4.00 post and handling. Choose any photograph included in this book. Your SEPIA print will be A4 in size, and mounted in a cream mount with burgundy rule line, overall size 14 x 11 inches.

Order additional Mounted Prints at HALF PRICE (only £7.49 each*)

If there are further pictures you would like to order, possibly as gifts for friends and family, purchase them at half price (no additional postage and handling required).

Have your Mounted Prints framed*

For an additional £14.95 per print you can have your chosen Mounted Print framed in an elegant polished wood and gilt moulding, overall size 16 x 13 inches (no additional postage and handling required).

> *** IMPORTANT!**
> **These special prices are only available if ordered using the original voucher on this page (no copies permitted) and at the same time as your free Mounted Print, for delivery to the same address**

Frith Collectors' Guild

From time to time we publish a magazine of news and stories about Frith photographs and further special offers of Frith products. If you would like 12 months FREE membership, please return this form.

Send completed forms to:
The Francis Frith Collection, Frith's Barn, Teffont, Salisbury, Wiltshire SP3 5QP

Voucher for FREE and Reduced Price Frith Prints

Picture no.	Page number	Qty	Mounted @ £7.49	Framed + £14.95	Total Cost
		1	Free of charge*	£	£
			£7.49	£	£
			£7.49	£	£
			£7.49	£	£
			£7.49	£	£
			£7.49	£	£

Please allow 28 days for delivery	*** Post & handling**	**£2.25**
Book Title	**Total Order Cost**	**£**

Please do not photocopy this voucher. Only the original is valid, so please cut it out and return it to us.

I enclose a cheque / postal order for £ . . . .
made payable to 'The Francis Frith Collection'
OR please debit my Mastercard / Visa / Switch / Amex card
(credit cards please on all overseas orders)

Number . . . .

Issue No(Switch only) . . . . .Valid from (Amex/Switch) . . . . . .

Expires . . . . Signature . . . .

Name Mr/Mrs/Ms . . . .

Address . . . .

. . . .

Postcode . . . . Daytime Tel No . . . .

Email Address . . . .

Valid to 31/12/04

The Francis Frith Collectors' Guild

Please enrol me as a member for 12 months free of charge.

Name Mr/Mrs/Ms . . . .

Address . . . .

. . . .

. . . .

. . . . Postcode . . . .

Would you like to find out more about Francis Frith?

We have recently recruited some entertaining speakers who are happy to visit local groups, clubs and societies to give an illustrated talk documenting Frith's travels and photographs. If you are a member of such a group and are interested in hosting a presentation, we would love to hear from you.

Our speakers bring with them a small selection of our local town and county books, together with sample prints. They are happy to take orders. A small proportion of the order value is donated to the group who have hosted the presentation. The talks are therefore an excellent way of fundraising for small groups and societies.

Can you help us with information about any of the Frith photographs in this book?

We are gradually compiling an historical record for each of the photographs in the Frith archive. It is always fascinating to find out the names of the people shown in the pictures, as well as insights into the shops, buildings and other features depicted.

If you recognize anyone in the photographs in this book, or if you have information not already included in the author's caption, do let us know. We would love to hear from you, and will try to publish it in future books or articles.

Our production team

Frith books are produced by a small dedicated team at offices in the converted Grade II listed 18th-century barn at Teffont near Salisbury, illustrated above. Most have worked with the Frith Collection for many years. All have in common one quality: they have a passion for the Frith Collection. The team is constantly expanding, but currently includes:

Jason Buck, John Buck, Douglas Burns, Ruth Butler, Angie Chick, Heather Crisp, Isobel Hall, Hazel Heaton, Peter Horne, James Kinnear, Tina Leary, Hannah Marsh, Sue Molloy, Kate Rotondetto, Dean Scource, Eliza Sackett, Terence Sackett, Sandra Sanger, Lewis Taylor, Shelley Tolcher, Clive Wathen and Jenny Wathen.